THE METROPOLITAN
RAILWAY

THE METROPOLITAN
RAILWAY

DAVID BOWNES

TEMPUS

Frontispiece: Metropolitan Railway A Class locomotive, No.26, pumping water from a flooded stretch of track near Farringdon Street station on 6 May 1915. This low-lying section of the Widened Lines was prone to flooding and on this occasion the railway was completely closed for two days. [1998/43459]

First published 2004

Tempus Publishing Limited
The Mill, Brimscombe Port,
Stroud, Gloucestershire, GL5 2QG
www.tempus-publishing.com

British Library Cataloguing in Publication Data.
A catalogue record for this book is available from the British Library.

ISBN 0 7524 3105 6

Typesetting and origination by Tempus Publishing Limited.
Printed in Great Britain.

Contents

The original crest of the Metropolitan Railway, combining the heraldic device of the City of London with a depiction of sub-surface trains entering and emerging from the tunnel. The legend 'We Work For All' highlights the philanthropic motives of the railway's promoters, and was later dropped. [2002/614]

Station staff at Neasden, c.1915. [2004/1540]

Introduction

The Metropolitan was the world's first underground railway. Opened in 1863 to provide a direct link between the City and the main line termini of Paddington, Euston and King's Cross, it showed that travel underground was a viable alternative to London's congested roads. Over the next twenty years the 'Met', in uneasy partnership with the District Railway, built an 'Inner Circle' of sub-surface railway within central London, nowadays known as the Circle line. It also jointly operated the Hammersmith & City and East London lines. But the Metropolitan was more than an urban transport system. By 1900 the network reached almost 50 miles north west of the company's headquarters at Baker Street, and served destinations in Middlesex, Hertfordshire and Buckinghamshire.

From the start, the Metropolitan regarded itself as a 'proper' railway, and certainly a cut above the deep level tubes that followed. This aspiration was expressed by a steady expansion northwards, first referred to as the extension line, but later known more grandly as 'the main line'. Like other main line railways, the Met offered a full range of goods and parcels services. Its surface stations, with their coal yards and sidings, were the same as hundreds of others throughout Britain, and even in central London passengers could send their parcels 'by Metropolitan'. In other aspects, too, the railway was unusual among its Underground rivals. For example, it operated two Pullman carriages for City businessmen and retained compartment coaches with luggage racks and coat hooks for its commuter trains. It also ran a mixture of 'fast' and 'stopping' trains to the suburbs, and referred to railway operating equipment by British names, rather than using the American terminology adopted by the new tubes from the early 1900s.

In popular terms, the railway is probably best remembered for the creation of suburban 'Metro-land', which is still served by the modern Metropolitan line. Spreading out from Willesden to Uxbridge, Watford and Amersham, the housing estates of Metro-land offered the promise of a modern home in semi-rural surroundings, yet well served by fast trains to London and the City. The Metro-land

Metropolitan Railway map, 1932. At its full extent,
the Metropolitan operated trains as far afield as New
Cross in south London and Brill in Buckinghamshire.
This map, which dramatically compresses the 50 miles
between Baker Street and Verney Junction,
concentrates on the central London network,
highlighting the various sports and recreation grounds
served by the Company.

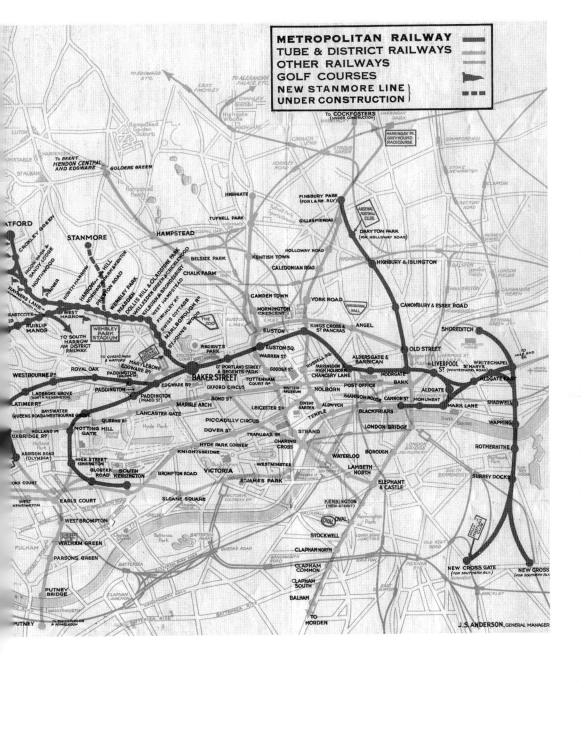

way of life was later immortalised in the poetry of John Betjeman and has provided inspiration for several writers, including Evelyn Waugh and Julian Barnes.

The Metropolitan was always an independently-minded company, shaped by a succession of strong-willed supporters, chairmen and managers. These included its philanthropic promoter Charles Pearson (1793-1862), the great railway mogul Sir Edward Watkin (1819-1901) and the less assuming, but no less important, general manager, Robert Selbie (1868-1930). These men helped to give a distinctive character and *esprit de corps* to the railway, which was echoed among its employees. None of this, however, could save the Metropolitan from forced amalgamation with the Underground Group (and other transport companies) to form the London Passenger Transport Board (LPTB) on 1 July 1933. Even so, the Met has retained some of its special character to the present day and, although no longer serving the furthest reaches of its earlier empire, can still boast the furthest destination on the London Underground.

This collection of photographs has been selected from the archives of London's Transport Museum and covers the operational life of the Metropolitan Railway from 1863-1933. Wherever possible, contemporary photographs are used, including some of the remarkable images commissioned to document the construction of the railway from 1862 to 1868. The selection also features photographs taken by London Transport in the mid-thirties to record its new assets. These images of locations, equipment and stock provide a comprehensive survey of the Metropolitan at the time of dissolution, albeit recorded at quiet moments to illustrate the subject to best effect.

The accompanying text can only provide an overview of the railway's history. Those interested in learning more about the subject are recommended to read Alan Jackson's definitive account, *London's Metropolitan Railway* (1986), which was a primary source for much of the caption information. The following titles were also consulted during the preparation of this book: *Metropolitan Electric Locomotives* by K.R. Beneset (1963), *The Romance of Metro land* by D. Edwards and R. Pigram (1979), *Metropolitan Steam Locomotives* by F. Goudie (1990), and *Metropolitan Railway Rolling Stock* by J.R. Snowdon (2001).

Copies of most prints reproduced in this publication may be purchased by writing to the address below and quoting the reference number in square brackets at the end of each caption. Personal visits to view the photographic collection, which covers all aspects of London's public transport, can be made by appointment.

David Bownes, Senior Curator
The Photo Library,
London's Transport Museum,
Covent Garden, WC2E 7BB
www.ltmuseum.co.uk

one

Building the
Railway

Charles Pearson (1793–1862) was Solicitor of the City of London and driving force behind the realisation of the Metropolitan Railway. His influential support was instrumental in raising the £1 million capital needed to build the initial line from Paddington to Farringdon Street. In addition to improving transport links between the City and main line termini, Pearson also stressed the social benefits of the scheme, which included the demolition of poor housing and provision of cheap fares to enable the 'working classes to reside in the adjacent country district'. Sadly, Pearson died just a few weeks before the railway opened to the public. [1998/84960]

Cross–section showing the innovative 'cut and cover' construction technique developed by the Metropolitan's engineers. Essentially, the road surface was lifted and a 'cutting' excavated below. Retaining walls, track and tunnel were then installed before the roadway was finally replaced, or 'covered' over. This drawing, made for the contractors Smith & Knight, also depicts the scaffolding needed to support adjoining buildings during construction. [1998/43547]

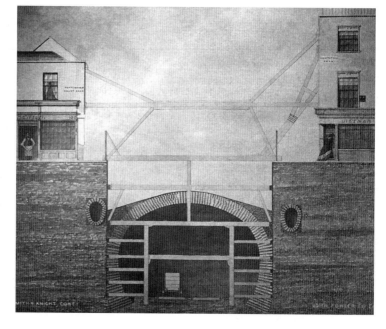

Above: Cut and cover construction in 1862. Much of the original route ran under the New Road (later renamed the Marylebone, Euston and Paddington roads). Excavation was made through the compacted debris of past ages, which in places lay in stratum up to 20ft deep and sometimes included human remains. [1998/75608]

Below: The exterior of the Metropolitan's original King's Cross station under construction in 1862. This section of the railway lay in open cutting and the station was designed along conventional railway lines, complete with elevated glass and iron train shed to help dispel the fumes and smoke of steam travel. [1998/37724]

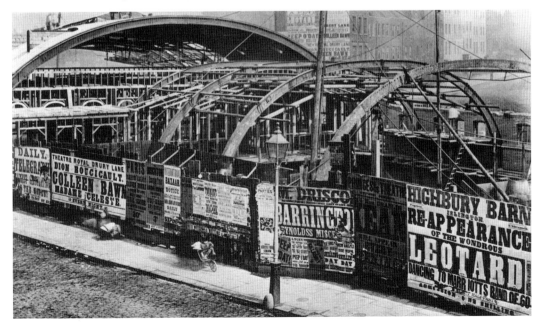

Above: Rail level photograph of King's Cross station nearing completion in 1862. The ghostly figures of workers too busy to pose for the photographer can be seen in the foreground. [1998/91234]

Right: Sir John Fowler (1817-98), Chief Engineer of the Metropolitan from its inception in 1852 to 1873. Fowler was one of the greatest civil engineers of his time and pioneered much of the technology used to build the 'Met' and subsequent sub-surface railways. [1998/84962]

'Fowler's Ghost' – the unofficial name given to the 'steamless' locomotive designed by John Fowler and built by Robert Stephenson & Co, seen here during a test run in May 1862. The engine was meant to reduce emissions underground (a requirement laid down by Parliament) by relying on preheated fire-bricks to maintain steam power when operating in the tunnel. The experiment was not a success, and modified locomotives were initially hired from the Great Western Railway to work the line instead. [1999/19984]

An inspection trip for shareholders and dignitaries at Edgware Road on 24 May 1862. John Fowler (in light coloured top hat, facing the camera) is seated next to the Chancellor of the Exchequer, William Gladstone. The initials 'S&K' on the side of the wagons stand for Smith & Knight, who were the contractors for the Bishops Road to Gower Street section of the railway. [1998/75478]

A contemporary illustration depicting the original seven stations of the Metropolitan opened on 10 January 1863. The new railway was an immediate success, with almost 40,000 passengers sampling the novelty of the eighteen-minute 'underground' journey on its first day of business.

A typical broad gauge Metropolitan train of 1863, depicted near Paddington. Carriages and locomotives were supplied by the Great Western, and fitted with condensing apparatus to reduce smoke emission. The track was laid with mixed broad and standard gauge rails to accommodate both the GWR and the Great Northern, which ran a standard gauge service from its junction with the Met at King's Cross to Farringdon Street. [1999/19986]

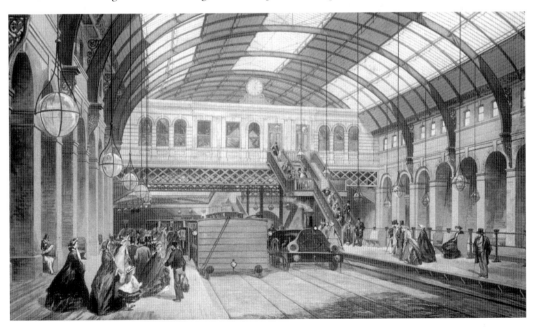

A bustling King's Cross station in the 1860s. This was the largest of the original stations, as extra space was needed by the GNR for its Farringdon service. The prominent gallery surmounted by a clock, linked stairs from each platform to the booking offices. [2001/15537]

One of the classic 4-4-0 tank engines ordered by the Metropolitan from 1864. Following a dispute with the GWR, the Met was forced to develop its own motive power. The result was the highly successful condensing tank locomotives designed by R.H. Burnett of the Manchester firm of locomotive builders, Beyer Peacock. Some sixty-six engines were supplied between 1864 and 1885, some of which survived in service until the 1930s. Originally finished in olive green, the engines were repainted maroon in the mid-1880s, which remained the standard colour for Met locomotives well into London Transport days. [1998/84908]

An atmospheric shot of Aldersgate (now Barbican) station taken at midnight on 22 April 1880 to show the effectiveness of the recently-introduced electric lighting. The station opened in 1865 as part of the extension from Farringdon to Moorgate. [1998/84029]

An early morning workmen's train at Moorgate Street in the 1860s. The Metropolitan was the first railway company in London to offer cheap fares to workmen. [1998/75443]

Artist's impression of a section of the City Widened Lines near Farringdon, built in the mid-1860s to connect Moorgate with the main lines of the GWR, GNR, London Chatham & Dover Railway and Midland Railway. To minimise disturbance, the section between King's Cross and Farringdon was built under the existing Metropolitan route, which was now carried on a dramatic skew bridge, known as the Ray Street grid-iron, seen here in the centre of the picture. [1998/87681]

Work in progress on the western extension at Praed Street, *c.*1866. A series of schemes was laid before Parliament in 1864 to complete an 'Inner Circle' of underground railway round the central area north of the Thames. The Metropolitan was authorised to extend westwards from Edgware Road to South Kensington, and eastwards from Moorgate to Tower Hill. The linking section was to be provided by the newly formed Metropolitan District Railway (MDR), which, despite its similar name, remained a separate undertaking. [1998/44718]

Cut and cover on the western extension. Where the route passed under existing streets, the normal method of construction was to close the road a few hundred yards at a time. Even so, the disruption caused was extensive and prolonged. [1998/84690]

Steam crane removing spoil at Craven Hill Gardens, Paddington, c.1867. The number of navvies hints at the enormous size of the workforce, which was managed by a consortium of eminent railway contractors, including Sir John Fowler, Peto & Betts, John Kelk and Waring Brothers. [1998/84911]

The dummy façade of 23/24 Leinster Gardens, Bayswater, built to conceal the railway where it passed under the road and to preserve the continuity of the street. The original houses were demolished during construction work in 1866. The façade remains to this day. [1998/86507]

Rear of 23/24 Leinster Gardens, showing an electric train entering the tunnel. The western extension passed through several fashionable residential districts, including Bayswater, Notting Hill and Kensington. Considerable effort was expended to ensure that the finished railway did not offend the sensibilities of local residents, and that stations were of suitable ornamental character. [1998/86505]

Building work in progress at Kensington (High Street), 1867. [1998/84721]

Street elevation of Paddington (Praed Street), as opened in October 1868. This style of station architecture, with minor modifications, was used for most of the Met stations built in the 1860s. [1998/85639]

Interior of Praed Street station looking to Edgware Road in 1868. The signal cabin and 'starter' signal can be seen at the end of the Up platform. [1998/38577]

Station staff pose with on-lookers outside the newly completed Bayswater station, 1868. [1998/84666]

Gloucester Road station, 1868. The station façade also advertises the Metropolitan District Railway, which began operating services from Gloucester Road in April 1869. [1998/74837]

The interior of Gloucester Road just prior to opening in 1868. Street level was reached via the central stairs leading to the booking office. [1998/84670]

Above: The original St John's Wood station adorned with Metropolitan Railway hoardings and posters. A nominally independent extension was opened from Baker Street to Swiss Cottage in 1868 with intermediate stations at St John's Wood Road and Marlborough Road. It was conceived as a 'feeder' line for the main system, but came to achieve far greater significance as a vehicle for northern expansion. The railway was formally absorbed by the Metropolitan in 1882. [1998/65358]

Right: Sir Myles Fenton, general manager of the Metropolitan from 1862-1879. Fenton was first appointed 'operating superintendent' on a salary of £500 a year. He left in 1880 to become general manager of the South Eastern Railway. [1998/20589]

Liverpool Street station in 1933. Progress eastwards was much slower than in west London. The extension to Bishopsgate (as Liverpool Street station was first known) was finished in 1875. The station was extensively rebuilt in 1911-2, with the new surface buildings shown here. [1998/69220]

Eastbound platform at Liverpool Street station in 1933. Passengers changed here for main line services from the city terminus of the Great Eastern Railway (later LNER).

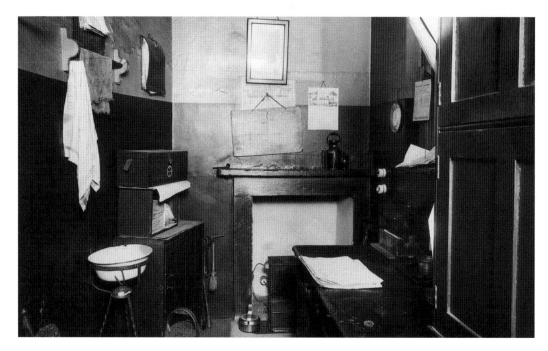

An unusual photograph of staff accommodation on the Metropolitan, in this case the 'Inspector's Room' at Liverpool Street. The basic facilities include a writing desk, washstand and primitive stove.

Aldgate station façade, c.1910. The station opened in 1876 as part of the eastern extension to complete the inner circle with the MDR at Mansion House. However, disagreements and rivalries between the two companies meant that the final link was not made until 1884. [1998/69199]

Mark Lane (later renamed Tower Hill) in 1897. The last section of the Inner Circle, from Aldgate to Mansion House, via Mark Lane, was jointly owned by the Met and MDR. [1998/84624]

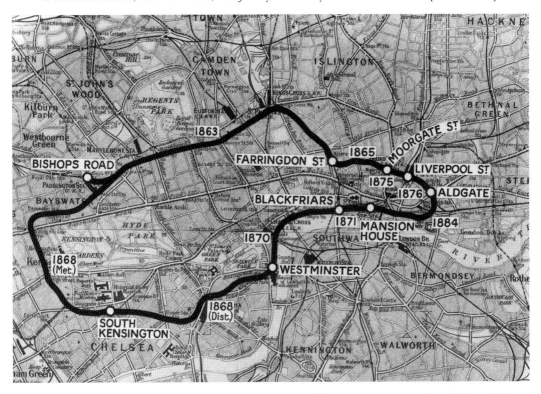

A map of the Inner Circle showing completion dates of the various sections from 1863 to 1884.

Above: From the mid-1860s the Metropolitan operated a number of horse bus feeder services to its inner London stations. This photograph of Regent Street shows a typical three-horse bus operated by the company in the 1880s, complete with distinctive Metropolitan Railway red umbrella. [1998/87632]

Opposite above: The defining image of steam underground – a Beyer Peacock 4-4-0, No.49, heading a Metropolitan passenger train at Aldgate in 1902. [1998/75664]

Opposite below: The Booking Office and entrance to Aldgate East in 1897. The station was opened in October 1884 on a jointly owned Met & MDR spur connecting the Circle with the East London Railway. [1998/84993]

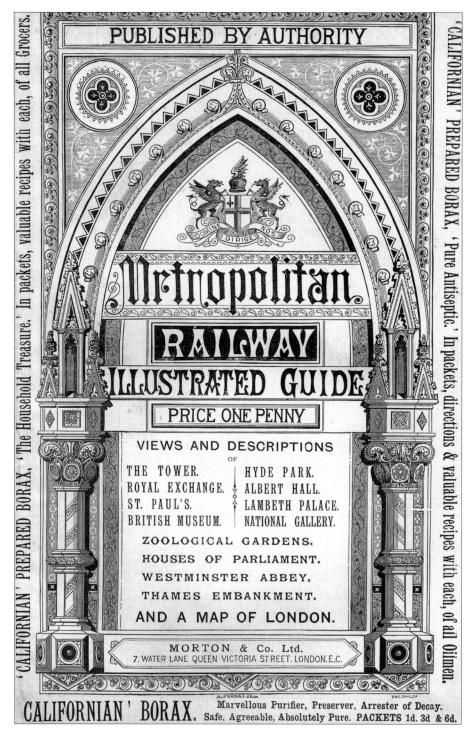

An *Illustrated Guide* published in the 1880s, after the completion of the Inner Circle. At this date, the focus of the company was the City and the attractions of central London. However, expansion northward would soon transform the Metropolitan both in size and aspiration.

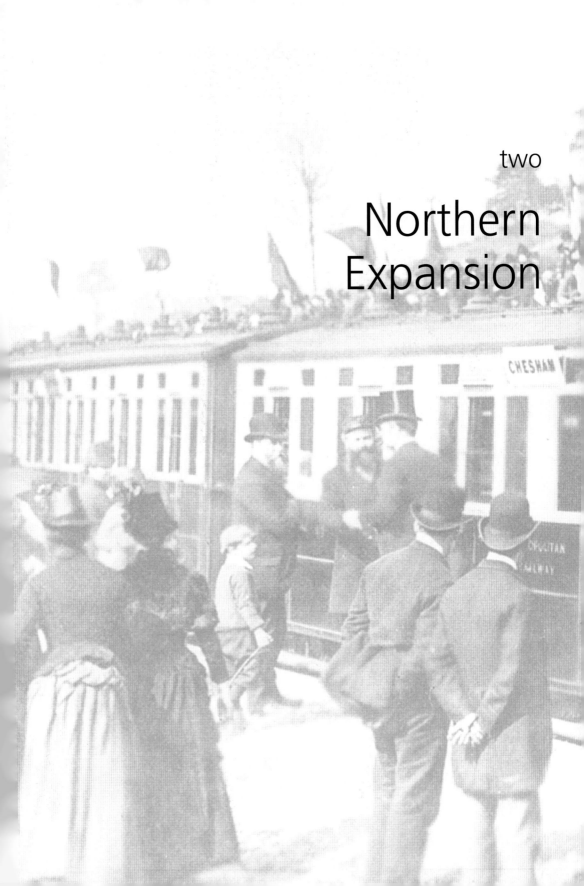

two

Northern Expansion

Sir Edward Watkin (1819-1901) was Chairman of the Metropolitan from 1872 to 1894 and driving force behind its expansion northwards. Watkin was the leading railway entrepreneur of his day, combining the chairmanship of the Met with that of the Manchester Sheffield & Lincolnshire Railway (MSLR) and the South Eastern Railway. He was also involved in the development of many smaller concerns, and envisaged a main line future for the MSLR stretching from Liverpool to Dover. The Met's eventual place in this scheme was to provide a way into London from the Midlands although its initial drive north was motivated by the need to increase passenger numbers.

The Metropolitan & St John's Wood Railway was extended from Swiss Cottage to Willesden Green in 1879. Intermediate stations were provided at Finchley Road, West Hampstead and Kilburn & Brondesbury. The original Willesden Green station, pictured here in 1910, was designed by A. McDermott and rebuilt in 1914. [1998/89721]

A street level view of Finchley Road station in 1910, complete with Metropolitan Railway horse-drawn parcel van. The scene is dwarfed by a massive hoarding advertising the recently-opened Wood Lane 'Exhibition Station' for the new White City exhibitions ground at Shepherd's Bush. [1998/75644]

Opened in August 1880, Harrow-on-the-Hill became the busiest station on the extension line. It had a locomotive, a carriage, and goods facilities, including the railway's first coal yard. In deference to the historic nature of the town, and the aristocratic patrons of Harrow School, a vaguely Queen Anne style of architecture was adopted for the station building. [1998/52140]

A Baker Street train hauled by A Class locomotive No.14 (originally named *Dido*) pulls out of Kingsbury and Neasden station in the 1890s en route for Harrow. The empty fields would soon be transformed by industrial and housing developments. [1998/61265]

Building work on the northern extension, thought to depict the construction of Neasden Depot, *c*.1882. A 290-acre site was acquired on the north side of the Extension line near Neasden for loco and carriage works to replace the original depot at Edgware Road. [1998/41325]

Aerial photograph of the completed Neasden works and power station early 1930s. The northern extension brought a vast increase in traffic to the Metropolitan. As the network grew, so too did the facilities at Neasden, which by 1909 employed nearly 900 staff, many of whom were housed by the company. [1998/86802]

An empty ballast train shunted by a Met locomotive at Neasden works, *c.*1934. [1998/55575]

Above, below and opposite above: Three photographs of Neasden works, *c.*1920. They show the Body Shop, Car Shed, and Saw Mills, together with a wide variety of goods vehicles, including cattle wagons and horse boxes. [2004/1541, 2004/1542 & 2004/1543]

Below: Railway workers' cottages in Aylesbury Street, Neasden. The first 102 cottages were completed in 1882 and graded for staff according to position within the company. More housing followed in the 1900s and 1920s, the latter designed by the company's architect, C.W. Clark. [2003/2500]

Above: Originally a contractor's engine, Nellie became part of the Met's modest fleet of Neasden based shunting locomotives in 1907. [1998/54791]

Below: An 0-6-0 saddletank shunting locomotive, of the type that once existed in thousands among the marshalling yards and industrial sidings of Britain. This example was one of two built by Peckett & Co for the Metropolitan in 1897 and 1899. They worked at Neasden Depot until 1960–61. [1998/87318]

Above: First Class carriage, No.346, built in 1887 by Craven Bros of Sheffield. These carriages, known as 'Jubilee' stock, were designed for use on the Inner Circle where they were formed into trains of nine cars, including two Second Class and two Firsts. They were finished in teak-panelled mahogany. More were ordered in 1889 and 1892, and later used on the extension to Aylesbury. [1998/69147]

Below: Opening day of the line to Chesham on 15 May 1889. The Met's northern expansion during the 1880s was rapid. Pinner was reached in 1885, followed by Rickmansworth in 1887. The section from Chalfont to Chesham was single line throughout. [2001/9512]

Exterior of Northwood station, situated between Pinner and Rickmansworth. This 1934 photograph shows the station under joint ownership of the Met & Great Central Joint Committee. The dreary façade is enlivened by an enormous poster advertising *Crosse and Blackwell's* grocery products. [1998/55917]

The northern extension required new locomotives, the first of which were built by Neilson & Co of Glasgow in 1891 and designated 'C' Class. They were also the first engines on the Met to be fitted with roofed cabs – to the relief of long suffering crews. No. 70 is seen here in works grey and fitted with condensing pipes (although the engines rarely worked the Inner Circle) where such apparatus was necessary. [1998/87448]

Cutting the first sod of the Aylesbury extension in 1890. From the mid 1880s, the focus of Watkin's plans for the Met was an extension to Aylesbury, from where it was would be possible to join with the MSLR via a number of proposed routes. The town was eventually reached on 1 September 1892. [1998/47679]

Amersham station in 1934. Originally part of the Aylesbury extension, Amersham now marks the outer limit of the modern day Metropolitan line. [1998/89754]

Left: The original 1892 signal box at Amersham, showing the distinctive pattern of name board used on the extension line. [2003/7260]

Below: The booking hall at Great Missenden station on the Aylesbury extension. The railway beyond Amersham was transferred to British Railways in 1961, and diesel services to Aylesbury are now operated by Chiltern Railways. [1998/69077]

Chesham station in 1934. With the opening of the extension from Chalfont Road (now Chalfont & Latimer) to Aylesbury, the railway to Chesham was relegated to branch line status. This view of the terminus, complete with signal box and water tower, is largely unchanged today. [1998/85058]

The means of reaching the MSLR proved to be the impoverished Aylesbury & Buckingham Railway (A&BR) – an independent railway opened in 1868 to connect Aylesbury with the LNWR at Verney Junction – purchased by the Metropolitan in 1891. The existing stations had to be rebuilt and the track doubled before main line operation could begin. Through trains from Baker Street to remote Verney Junction (depicted here in 1936) began on 1 January 1897. [1998/36772]

The connection with Watkin's MSLR was made near Quainton Road, now the Buckinghamshire Railway Centre's home. This enabled the MSLR to complete its main line from Nottinghamshire to London, with running powers over the Metropolitan to Marylebone, via a junction near Finchley Road. Quainton Road was also the terminus of a branch line to Brill, seen on the right. [1998/84261]

Typical of the rebuilt stations on the A&BR was Granborough Road, seen here shortly after passing into London Transport ownership. [1998/84242]

Westcott station, one of the intermediate stops on the rural Brill branch. The line was built as a tramway to serve the Duke of Buckingham's estate. Its potential for possible westward expansion was recognised by Watkin, who ensured that it passed into Metropolitan hands during the 1890s and was rebuilt to railway operating standards. [1998/84862]

A typical 'mixed goods' train on the Brill Tramway in pre-Metropolitan days, hauled by Aveling & Porter engine, No.1. [1998/87679]

One of three Manning Wardle 0-6-0STs, *Brill No.2*, purchased during the 1890s to work the rebuilt Brill branch. [1998/87678]

The end of the line: Brill station in August 1935 with a mixed goods train from Quainton Road. At this date, the line was still operated by London Transport, although it would close before the end of the year. [1998/84674]

'D' Class locomotive No.75, one of six introduced in 1894-95 on the Aylesbury-Verney Junction and Brill lines. The 'D' Class engines were not a great success, and were withdrawn by 1923. [1998/75645]

A characteristic extension line train of the 1900s, consisting of six 'Ashbury' 1898 stock carriages and a four wheel luggage van, hauled by 'E' Class locomotive, No.77. The 'E' Class were specifically designed for the Metropolitan and worked the majority of main line services from 1896 until the appearance of the 'G' Class 0-6-4 tanks in 1915-6. [1998/75658]

Above: 'Watkin's Tower', the unfinished centrepiece of a planned leisure park, can be seen above the trees at Wembley Park *c.*1905. Watkin bought the park in 1889, believing that its proximity to London would make it the perfect venue for a complex of rail-served restaurants, theatres, shops and dance halls. The first level of the tower (to have been the tallest in Europe) was opened in 1896, but public interest dwindled and the money ran out. Nicknamed 'Watkin's Folly', the tower was demolished in 1907 and the site later redeveloped as the world famous Wembley stadium. [1998/50349]

Right: A handbill announcing the public opening of the Uxbridge branch on 4 July 1904. The seven and a half mile railway served a predominantly rural area and joined the main line at Harrow. A single intermediate station was provided at Ruislip.

Below: The official opening of the Uxbridge branch on 30 June 1904. A special train, seen here at Ruislip, ran from Baker Street to South Harrow and Uxbridge, with luncheon served in a marquee in Uxbridge station yard. The locomotive is 0-4-4T No.1, lavishly decorated with flags, foliage and white washed coal. It survives as the only operational Met steam engine in preservation, based at the Buckinghamshire Railway Centre at Quainton Road. [1998/87555]

Opposite below: By 1900, goods traffic on the extension line was increasing beyond the capabilities of the 'D' and 'E' Class locomotives. In response, the Met ordered four powerful 0-6-2 tank engines (designated 'F' Class) from the Yorkshire Engine Company in 1901 at a cost of £3,350 each. [2003/4635]

METROPOLITAN RAILWAY.

OPENING OF EXTENSION

TO

UXBRIDGE

JULY 4th, 1904.

Ordinary Fares

AND

Season Ticket Rates

TO

CITY & WEST END STATIONS.

General Manager's Office,
32, Westbourne Terrace, W.   A. C. ELLIS,
30th June, 1904.   *General Manager.*

Uxbridge Station on 26 April 1934. The terminus was laid out for easy conversion into a through station, as there were plans to extend the line towards High Wycombe. [1998/88584]

The City Goods Depot in Vine Street. With the increase in goods traffic, the Metropolitan needed a central London depot for deliveries and collection. The Vine Street site, near Farringdon station, was opened in November 1909. Local cartage was provided by the railway, as illustrated by the horse drawn delivery van in this photograph. [1998/68452]

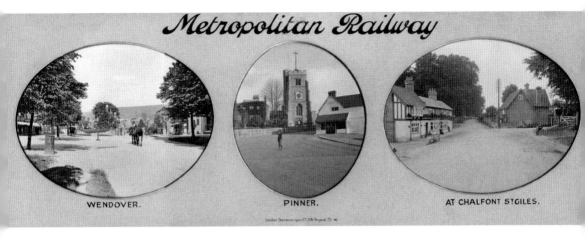

Metropolitan Railway

WENDOVER.   PINNER.   AT CHALFONT ST GILES.

A photographic carriage panel, presenting a bucolic image of villages served by the northern extension, *c*.1910. [2000/12135]

An official Metropolitan Railway postcard promoting the rural attractions of Batchworth Heath near Northwood station, *c*.1910. By this date, the Met had begun to develop plots of vacant land next to its northern stations, a process that would eventually lead to the creation of 'Metro-land'. [2003/15713]

The illuminated interchange sign at Baker Street station, indicating destinations on the extension line, photographed in 1957. The backlit lettering, in a serifed Metropolitan typeface, is in marked contrast to the familiar Johnson sans serif typeface of the London Transport 'Way Out' sign (top right). [1998/60726]

three

Electrification

Above: Neasden power station, *c.*1904. The problem of ventilation on the Inner Circle had never been fully resolved, and with the advent of viable electric traction after 1890, it was clear that the days of steam underground were numbered. Following experiments (and arguments) over electrification systems with the District Railway, the Met chose Neasden for the site of its generating station, which from 1905 supplied electricity for Circle and Uxbridge services. [1998/49475]

Right: The turbine hall at Neasden, *c.*1905. The power station had a capacity of 10,500kw, or 14,075 horse power, provided by British Westinghouse turbo generators. [2002/9509]

Stokers and foremen posed against the 'first turbine' to be installed at Neasden, *c.*1905. [2004/1544]

The trial run of the new electric stock between Baker Street and Uxbridge on 13 December 1904. The assembled dignitaries include the Chairman, Lord Aberconway, and the General Manager, A.C. Ellis. Public services commenced on Sunday 1 January 1905. [1998/61311]

Above: A typical 1905 stock electric train, comprised of four trailers flanked by two motor cars. The design of these early carriages was very American, reflecting the source of much of the technology used. [1998/87954]

Right: The final version of the Metropolitan crest, incorporating the coats of arms of the City of London and the counties of Middlesex, Buckinghamshire and Hertfordshire, surmounted by a clenched fist and sparks to celebrate the power and efficiency of electric traction. This device was used on everything from uniform buttons to rolling stock and locomotives. [2003/4389]

A 3rd Class motor car No.30, showing the luggage compartment situated immediately behind the driver's cab. This was a necessary addition for longer-distance travel, and reflected the Metropolitan's aspirations to main line, rather than just commuter, status. [1998/87953]

Motor car No.40 photographed at Neasden in 1934. Passenger loading problems resulted in the installation of a central double doorway to the original 1905 stock. [1998/68385]

Above: Electric locomotive No.6 at the head of a goods train near Farringdon Street Goods Depot, *c.*1910. [1998/87812]

Opposite above: Exterior of Aldersgate Street (now Barbican) station in 1933 advertising 'Electric Trains To All Parts of London'. The electrification of the Inner Circle was completed in 1905. [1998/89304]

Opposite below: In 1906 the Metropolitan acquired ten camel-backed locomotives from the Metropolitan Amalgamated Carriage Company, fitted with Westinghouse electrical equipment. They were initially used to haul heavy passenger trains on the Baker Street to Uxbridge service. No.2 is seen here with crew and station staff at Neasden in the 1900s. [1998/87811]

Another view of No.2, this time at Harrow-on-the-Hill with a six-car train for Liverpool Street, 1921. Although reasonably successful operationally, the locomotives' camel-backed design and centrally placed controls made visibility poor and driving awkward. [1998/87810]

The Metropolitan's second batch of electric locomotives was fitted with British Thompson-Houston equipment, and entered service in 1907 numbered 11-20. The 'box-cab' design was a great improvement over the earlier camel-backed layout, although neither type was problem-free and all twenty locomotives were replaced in the 1920s.

An 1898 Bogie stock coach after conversion to electric working in 1906. Following electrification, a number of previously steam-hauled carriages were rebuilt as motor coaches. They were used primarily on the Uxbridge, and later Stanmore, branches. [1998/69140]

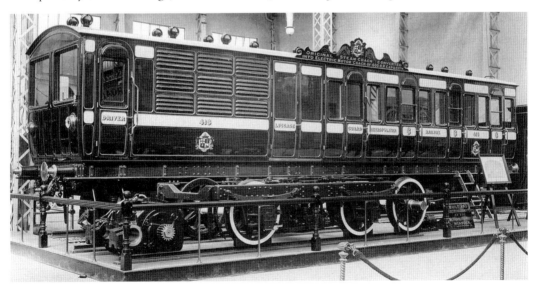

Converted Bogie stock motor coach 418 displayed in its original livery at the 1924 British Empire Exhibition at Wembley. The Metropolitan was clearly very pleased with the success of its conversion programme, much of which was undertaken at Neasden works. [1998/62822]

Above: The sister car, *Mayflower*, at Baker Street station. The two cars ran until October 1939 and had the distinction of being the first electrically hauled Pullmans in Europe. [1998/88233]

Opposite above: The interior of a signal box at Harrow in March 1938. For many years, Harrow marked the northernmost limit of Metropolitan electrification and the point where steam replaced electric for the remainder of extension line services from Baker Street. [2002/5352]

Opposite below: One of the Metropolitan's two First Class Pullman cars, *Galatea,* in its final crimson lake livery, photographed at Neasden Depot in 1934. Pullman services were introduced in 1910 to and from Amersham, Chesham and Verney Junction. It was seen as a means of retaining wealthy City commuters and countering the threat posed by rival GCR services out of Marylebone. [1998/88235]

Above: Both Pullmans offered a fully stocked bar and a wide range of expensively priced refreshments. The service was never strongly patronised, but was retained for its prestige value. [1998/88115]

Opposite above: The interior of a Metropolitan Pullman, looking from the pantry end. Passengers paid the full First Class fare plus a supplement of 6*d* for journeys anywhere between Aldgate and Rickmansworth and one shilling beyond the latter. [1998/62881]

Opposite below: The success of the electrification programme prompted the purchase of a further ten six-car trains of saloon stock, plus three spare motor cars, in 1913. The cars were essentially a development of the tried and tested 1905 stock, updated with elliptical roofs and central sliding doors as standard – as illustrated here by 3rd Class trailer No.80. [1998/69162]

Above: The 1921-stock 3rd class trailer 103. Some fifty-nine cars were ordered after the First World War for use on the Circle. Similar in design to the 1913 stock, the new cars benefited from the experiments in passenger loading and had improved access via three sets of repositioned sliding doors. [1998/68358]

Opposite above: Interior of a 1913 stock 3rd class trailer, August 1934. [1998/46235]

Opposite below: The 1st class driving trailer No.55 was part of an experimental six-car train rebuilt from existing stock in 1919 to compare the passenger loading times of improved 'slam' door carriages with centre-doored saloon stock. The 'Hustle Train', as it became known, was only partially successful as the narrow door openings caused congestion at peak times. It remained in service in its rebuilt form until 1931. [1998/75674]

Above: After the war, the Metropolitan embarked on a programme of rebuilding its existing fleet of electric locomotives with more powerful motors. However, the scheme proved far too costly and instead an order was placed with Metropolitan-Vickers Ltd for twenty new engines, each fitted with four 300hp traction motors. Thirteen of the locos can be seen here under construction at the Vickers Works in Barrow-in-Furness, 1921. [1998/62836]

Opposite above: 'Metro-Vick' locomotive No.17 (later named *Florence Nightingale*) in original scarlet livery with straw-coloured numerals and lettering flanked by the Company crest.

Opposite below: A sectioned view of No.15 (later named *Wembley 1924*) at the British Empire Exhibition, 1924. [1998/88250]

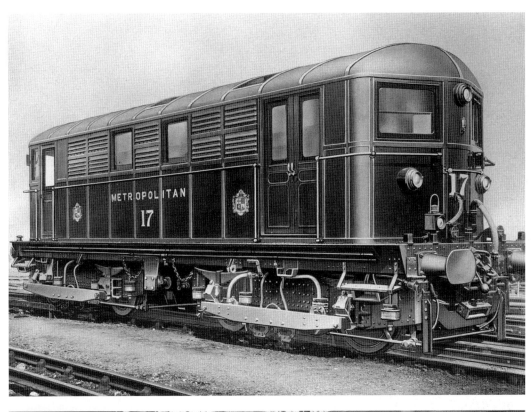

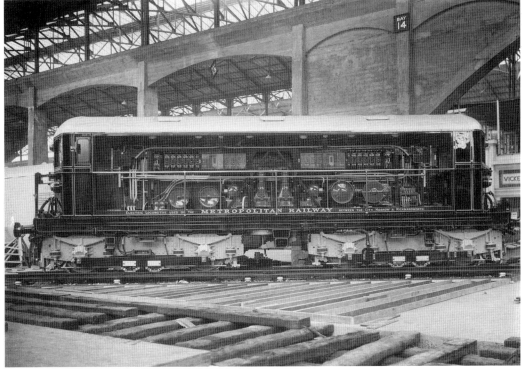

Above: The No.2 *Oliver Cromwell* (later renamed *Thomas Lord*) about to depart Rickmansworth with a passenger train for Aldgate in August 1934. The Main Line was electrified from Harrow to Rickmansworth in 1925, where the changeover from electric to steam traction took as little as three minutes. In this photograph, H Class steam locomotive No.104 can be seen returning to the lay-by siding at the north end of the station having powered the train from Verney Junction. [1998/88883]

Opposite above: Promotional brochure produced by Metropolitan Vickers Ltd celebrating the electrification of the Metropolitan Railway to Rickmansworth and the success of its own locomotive design in 1925.

Opposite below: MV stock motor coach No.207. The MV and MW motor cars were introduced in 1927 for Main Line passenger services. They were fitted with four 275hp motors, making them the most powerful multiple-unit vehicles in Europe at the time. The MV and MW stock was designed with compartment, rather than saloon, accommodation, partly because of passenger preference for this type of seating on extension line services. [1998/88798]

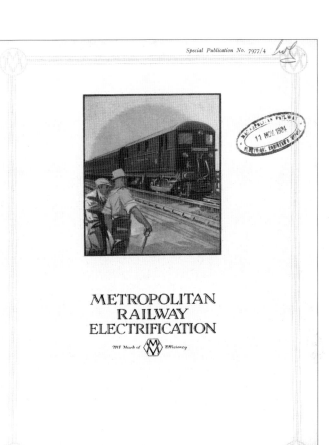

METROPOLITAN
RAILWAY
ELECTRIFICATION

THE Mark of **M** Efficiency

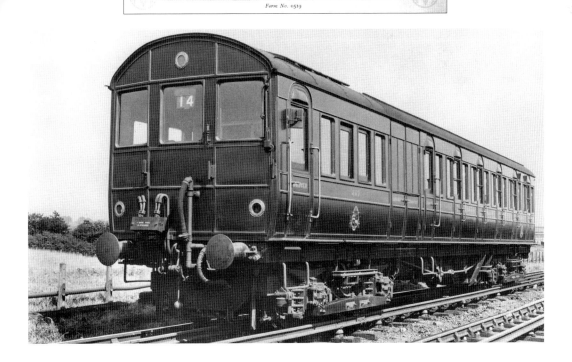

An MV stock train approaching Wembley Park, with the twin chimneys of Neasden power station dominating the skyline. The long platform on the left was built for the Empire Exhibitions of 1924 and 1925 and named 'Wembley Park Exhibition Station'.

Interior of Neasden Depot car shed in August 1937, showing four trains of ex MV, MW and 1913 Stock. [1998/20442]

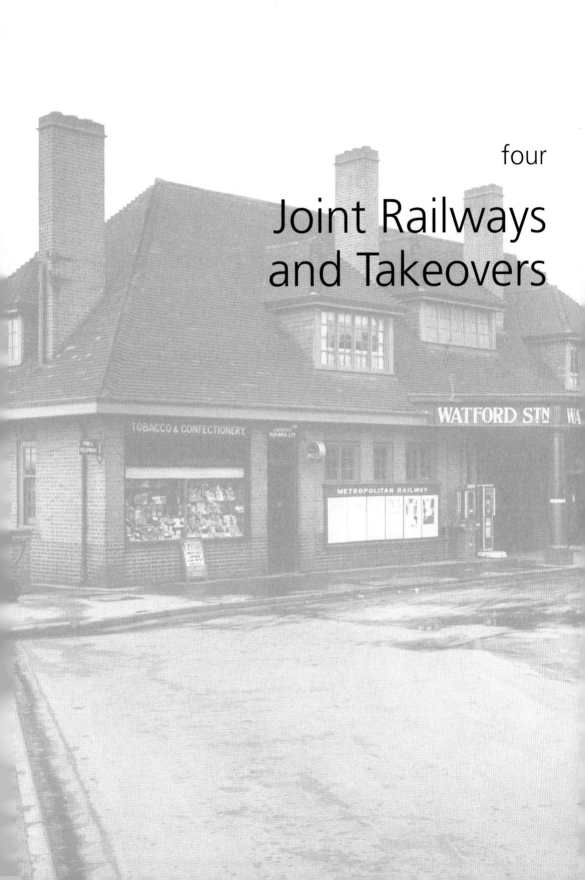

four

Joint Railways and Takeovers

The Hammersmith & City Railway was promoted to develop commuter traffic between west London and the City. It joined the Metropolitan via a junction with the Great Western near Paddington. From its launch in 1864, the H&CR was operated by the Metropolitan and Great Western railways and quickly passed into their joint ownership. This monogram was used on the sides of rolling stock. [1998/41314]

Metropolitan Railway A Class locomotive No.4, *Mercury,* at the head of a four-car set of eight-wheel rigid coaches, photographed at Hammersmith station *c.*1868. The H&C was originally built to accommodate both broad and standard gauge trains. [1998/60530]

METROPOLITAN & Gᵀ· WESTERN RAILWAYS.

On MONDAY, 2nd APRIL, 1888,

A NEW SERVICE OF

TWO HORSE OMNIBUSES

WILL COMMENCE RUNNING ON WEEK DAYS

BETWEEN

HAMMERSMITH

STATION AND

WHITE HART HOTEL,

BARNES

EVERY **20** MINUTES

AS UNDER:—

From BARNES (White Hart Hotel).		From HAMMERSMITH STATION.	
First 'Bus ...	8. 0 a.m.	First 'Bus ...	8.30 a.m.
Last „ ...	7.40 p.m.	Last „ ...	8.10 p.m.

Fares
{
Between Hammersmith Station & the Red Lion 2d.
The Red Lion and White Hart Hotel, Barnes ...2d.
All the Way ....3d.

PADDINGTON, W., *March*, 1888.   BY ORDER.

Waterlow & Sons Limited, Printers, London Wall, London.

Left: The H&C Joint Committee first ran horse buses to Barnes in 1878, having previously operated similar services to Shepherd's Bush and Turnham Green. The 'two horse omnibus' that is advertised here was retained until April 1899. [1998/75725]

Below: A Hammersmith train hauled by A Class locomotive No.55 at Aldgate towards the end of the nineteenth century. The earliest H&C trains had terminated at Farringdon Street for the City. Services were later extended via connections with the West London, East London and London & South Western railways, to destinations such as New Cross and Richmond. [1998/87306]

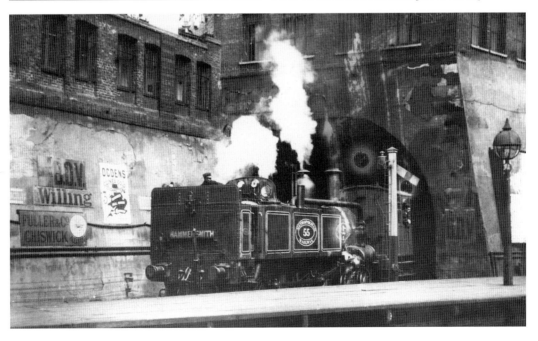

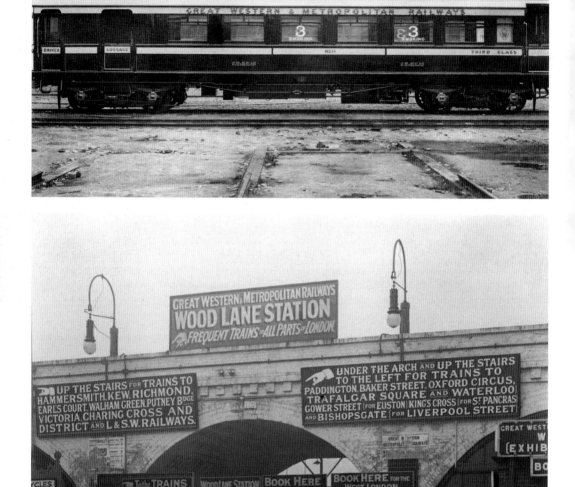

Above: Hammersmith station and forecourt in 1933. The station was substantially rebuilt between 1907 and 1909 to the plans of the GWR architect P.E. Culverhouse. [1998/56074]

Opposite above: H&CR 3rd Class electric motor car in original varnished teak and white livery. The railway was electrified in 1906. [1998/88790]

Opposite below: The entrance to Wood Lane station opened in May 1908 to serve the Franco-British Exhibition at White City. This photograph, taken around 1910, displays the bewildering array of information signs which would have greeted the passenger. By this date, services were sufficiently extended for the H&CR to boast 'Frequent Trains to All Parts of London'. [1998/87025]

Staff at Neasden paint shop pose during the renovation of Hammersmith & City electric stock, c.1923. The Metropolitan gradually assumed control of the H&CR by agreements with the GWR in 1913 and 1923, including responsibility for rolling stock and power supply. The Joint Committee survived until the nationalisation of the railways in 1948. [2004/1545]

Wapping station on the East London Railway, showing the entrance to the Thames Tunnel, c.1870. The ELR was formed in 1865 to connect the main line railways of south London with those of the north and was initially worked by the London Brighton & South Coast Railway. The completed route between Shoreditch and New Cross incorporated the pioneering Thames Tunnel, originally built for pedestrian use by Sir Marc Brunel. The Metropolitan became involved in the operation of the ELR in the 1880s, mainly due to the influence of Sir Edward Watkin who was Chairman of both companies. [1998/84882]

The entrance to Wapping station. From 1882, management of the ELR was vested in a joint committee consisting of the LB&SC, South Eastern, London, Chatham & Dover, District and Metropolitan Railways, later joined by the Great Eastern Railway. [1998/56043]

St Mary's (Whitechapel Road), c.1913. A physical link with the Circle was opened in 1884 from a junction south of the ELR's Whitechapel station westwards to St Mary's station, jointly operated by the Metropolitan and District Railways. [1998/66037]

Above and below: The exterior and booking hall of Shadwell station, opened in 1876 between Wapping and Shoreditch. The station was built on a spring and as recently as the Second World War, passengers could request to 'take the waters' which, despite flowing from a retaining wall, were believed to have health-giving properties. [2004/1546 and 1998/65118]

A Metropolitan electric train awaits the off at New Cross, one of two stations bearing the same name which connected the ELR with the SER and LB&SCR, *c.*1914. The ELR was not fully electrified until 1913. This delay, compared with the 1905 electrification of the Circle, had resulted in the temporary withdrawal of Metropolitan and District railway services. From 1914 the Metropolitan operated all passenger services. [1998/86569]

Shoreditch, which opened in 1876, marked the northern limit of the ELR. Following the 1923 'Grouping' of main line railway companies, the management of the ELR was taken over by the Metropolitan, Southern Railway, London & North Eastern Railway and Underground Group, neatly represented by the four-poster boards adorning the station façade. It was formally absorbed into the SR in 1925, but managed on a day-to-day basis by the Metropolitan from 1921 until 1933. [1998/55319]

ONE·PENNY.

METROPOLITAN & GREAT·CENTRAL
JOINT~RAILWAY
Illustrated·Guide 1910.

Left: The Metropolitan & Great Central Joint Committee (M&GCJC) was formed in April 1906 to manage the northern extension between Harrow South and Verney junctions, including the Brill and Chesham branches. The Great Central Railway, as the MSLR was known from 1897, had existing running powers over the line from Finchley Road to Quainton Road. This new arrangement enabled closer working relations and shared costs. It also ensured that the GCR continued to use the route for its northern expresses, rather than seeking a new approach into central London. Each company provided its own train services.

Below: A Metropolitan electric hauled passenger train approaching Willesden Green pursued by a Great Central express, *c.*1910. To ease congestion, the line between Harrow South and Finchley Road was doubled in 1901 for GCR services to Marylebone.

Above: The approach to Wendover station, dominated by a vast poster board proclaiming its joint ownership, in 1934. Management of the M&GCJC was initially rotated between each company for a period of five years. It was later agreed that the GCR would maintain the section north of Great Missenden, with the Metropolitan in charge of the section to the south. [1998/56670]

Below: G Class 0-6-4T *Robert H. Selbie* in original livery at Neasden, *c*.1920. The G Class was introduced in 1915-16 for passenger and goods traffic on the northern extension. The locomotives, numbered 94-97, were built by the Yorkshire Engine Company and named *Lord Aberconway* (Chairman of the Metropolitan), *Robert H. Selbie* (General Manager), *Charles Jones* (Chief Mechanical Engineer) and *Brill*. [1998/87439]

Above: The forecourt of Aylesbury station in 1934. The original station was built by the GWR–owned Wycombe Railway, and later shared by the Aylesbury and Buckingham Railway from 1868. Following the latter's take-over by the Met and the formation of the M&GCJC, the station was jointly managed by the Metropolitan, GCR and GWR and rebuilt in 1924. A road motor van owned by all three companies can be seen collecting parcels outside the main entrance. [1998/56658]

Below: An extension line passenger train powered by H Class locomotive No.107 at Rickmansworth, in August 1934. Kerr Stuarts supplied eight of these engines in 1920-21, primarily for passenger services north of Rickmansworth – the limit of Metropolitan electrification after 1925. [1998/68685]

Left: Interior of a 1910 steam stock 3rd Class compartment carriage, complete with overhead luggage rack – still retained by modern Metropolitan main line trains. The diagram in the central frame shows the M&GCJC route from Rickmansworth to Verney Junction, including the Brill and Chesham branches. [1998/63647]

Below: North Harrow was opened by the M&GCJC in 1915 in response to suburban development, and extensively rebuilt to a Metropolitan Railway design between 1929 and 1931. By this date, the Met had assumed responsibility for the management of the Joint Committee, although the interests of the GCR continued to be represented by its post-war successor, the London & North Eastern Railway. The M&GCJC retained its identity following the creation of London Transport in 1933, and was not dissolved until 1948 when it was divided between British Railways and LT. [1998/86865]

Above: Metropolitan Railway K Class locomotive, No.115, photographed in the early thirties at the head of a goods train near Verney Junction. The powerful K Class 2-6-4 Tanks were introduced in 1925 for heavy freight, enabling the working of fewer, longer, trains over the Joint section. In common with the G and H Classes, the K Class engines were sold to the LNER in November 1937 when the latter company took over the responsibility for Metropolitan line steam hauled services from London Transport. [1998/25047]

Below: The Great Northern & City Railway (GN&CR) was promoted to link the Great Northern at Finsbury Park with Moorgate, enabling GNR trains to run directly into the city. However, by the time the line opened in 1904 the GNR had withdrawn its support, so that the GN&CR became an isolated tube line, only three and half miles long and heavily dependent on peak-hour traffic. It was taken over by the Metropolitan in July 1913, ostensibly to protect the lucrative traffic passing over the City Widened Lines, which would be threatened if the GN&CR fell into GNR hands. The Met also hoped to extend the railway as a feeder for the Inner Circle. [1998/83980]

GREAT NORTHERN & CITY TUBE

THE ONLY QUICK ROUTE
BETWEEN
NORTH & SOUTH LONDON.

GREAT NORTHERN AND CITY TUBE. STEEL MOTOR COACH.

FINSBURY PARK TO MOORGATE IN 13 MINUTES.

NO WAITING!! TRAINS EVERY 2 or 3 Mins.

THROUGH BOOKINGS WITH:

GREAT NORTHERN RLY, METROPOLITAN, CITY & SOUTH LONDON RLY, AND LONDON BRIGHTON & SOUTH COAST RLY

	FIRST TRAIN	LAST TRAIN
MOORGATE TO FINSBURY PK	a.m. 5·55	p.m. 11·20
Sundays	11·30	11·15
FINSBURY PK TO MOORGATE	5·40	11·10
Sundays	11·15	11·5

——— STATIONS ———

FINSBURY PARK, for Seven Sisters Rd Stroud Green Rd
GREAT NORTHERN RLY. (stairs & lift connection) Trams to Wood Green & Tottenham.
DRAYTON PARK, for Highbury Hill and Holloway
HIGHBURY for Upper St, Highbury Fields and North London Ry
   Trams to Agricultural Hall, Angel and Highgate
ESSEX ROAD, for New North Rd., Canonbury, Agricultural Hall
OLD STREET, for City Rd., Aldersgate St., Shoreditch, Goswell Rd.,
   Hoxton; Trams to Commercial Rd and Poplar
MOORGATE for Bank, The Metropolitan Ry, The City & South London
Tube (for the Central London Tube and the Brighton & South Coast Ry)

COMFORTABLE AND SPEEDY.

NO STRAPHANGING GOOD VENTILATION.

Above: GN&CR gate stock, built by Brush Electrical Engineering and powered by British Thomson-Houston equipment. The GN&CR was the only deep-level tube built with 16ft diameter tunnels to take standard main line rolling stock. [1998/58281]

Below: The interior of Drayton Park signal box with the signalling diagram and frame, *c.*1933. The GN&CR operated a unique automatic signalling system only requiring manual operation from the two termini, although this box was staffed when it was necessary to shunt or divide trains. [1998/67187]

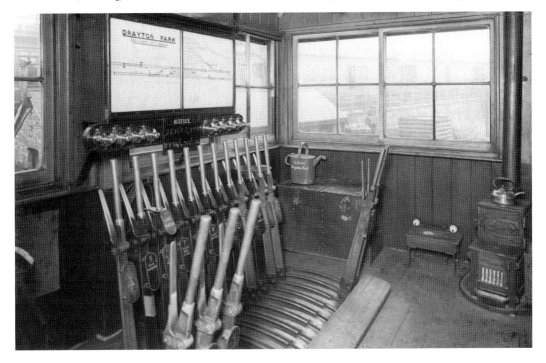

The GN&CR's solitary shunting engine, an ex-Metropolitan 1906 camel-backed locomotive, at Drayton Park Depot, April 1934. It remained in service until 1948. [1998/62108]

First Class trailer No.53 after passing into Metropolitan ownership. Some 1st Class accommodation was introduced by the status conscious Met from 1915. The GN&CR was renamed the Northern City by London Transport in the 1930s and eventually transferred to British Railways in October 1975. [1998/88094]

The cramped interior of Moorgate signal cabin, built into the curve of the tunnel wall. The two paraffin lamps in the foreground were for hand signalling and could display red, green and clear light. [2002/13479]

BLOTTER

WHY YOU SHOULD TRAVEL METRO.

CONTINUOUS ELECTRIC TRAIN SERVICE — SPEEDY & COMFORTABLE TRAVEL

3-MONTHLY METRO. SEASON TICKET RATES FROM WATFORD STATION

TYPICAL EXAMPLE OF THE SAVING OF A METRO. SEASON TICKET

TO	1st Class 3 mths. £ s. d.	3rd Class 3 mths. £ s. d.
Kilburn & Brondesbury ..	6 5 3	4 1 3
Baker Street ..	7 6 3	4 6 9
Euston Square ..	7 6 3	4 6 9
King's Cross & St. Pancras ..	7 16 0	4 16 0
Liverpool Street ..	8 2 3	4 19 6
Paddington (Bishops Road and Praed St.)	7 11 6	5 0 6

Monthly and Weekly "Seasons" at low rates are also issued.

	1st Class £ s. d.	3rd Class £ s. d.
Cost of taking Return Ticket daily for three months, between Watford and Liverpool Street..	30 11 0	17 11 0
Cost of Quarterly Ticket	8 2 3	4 19 6
Saving to Season Ticket holder ..	22 8 9	12 11 6

JOURNEY TIMES OF METRO. TRAINS FROM WATFORD STATION

Baker Street	34	Minutes
Euston Square	40	,,
King's Cross	42	,,
Moorgate	48	,,
Liverpool Street	50	,,
Aldgate	52	,,

FIRST AND LAST TRAINS BETWEEN WATFORD AND CITY STATIONS

FIRST TRAIN

Watford to City Stations .. .. .. 6.26 a.m.

LAST TRAIN

Watford to City Stations .. .. 11.41 p.m.

A continuous service of electric trains is maintained, in both directions, between these hours.

Other information can be obtained from Commercial Manager, Baker St. Station, N.W.1

Above: A promotional blotter advertising the newly opened Metropolitan & LNER branch line to Watford, 1925. The branch joined the main line at Rickmansworth and Moor Park, and was managed by the Watford Joint Railway Committee, made up of representatives from the two parent companies.

Below: Watford Junction signal box, Met & LNER Joint. The signalling diagram shows the triangular junction between the branch and the main line.

A platform view of Croxley Green on the Watford branch, September 1944. The station, renamed Croxley in 1949, served a growing suburban district and was equipped with an extensive goods yard. [1998/66326]

Watford station, designed by the Metropolitan's architect C.W. Clark. In form, the station was very similar to Croxley Green, with red brick walls under steeply-pitched, multi-chimneyed roofs. It was situated at the extreme edge of the town, with the result that passenger traffic was at first disappointing, although later housing developments at nearby Cassiobury Park did much to improve figures. [1998/74898]

The Metropolitan introduced a bus service from Watford station to the town centre in 1927. The fleet of four Albion motorbuses was initially owned and crewed by the company. Within a short time the service was carrying up to 500 passengers a day. It became part of the London Passenger Transport Board on 1 October 1933. [1999/28830]

five

Metro-Land

The route to suburbia – An Aylesbury-bound passenger train departing Baker Street, c.1900. In building the northern extension, the Metropolitan acquired large tracts of rural land that later became the setting for the line-side housing estates of Metro-land. Uniquely among railway companies, the Met was able to develop these estates itself due to dubious privileges won during its early property battles with the City.

A Neasden train passing new housing near Willesden Green, c.1895. The Met's first venture into suburban development was the 400-acre Willesden Park Estate, built during the 1880s. Property development was managed by a subsidiary company, the Surplus Lands Committee, which had the power to undertake new purchases in the name of the railway company. [1998/87794]

CECIL PARK ESTATE, PINNER.

IF you are seeking a house on this popular Estate please send your name and address when they will be filed and you will be advised in due course when any houses are available.

The rents vary from £45 to £70 a year and the purchase prices from £485 leasehold and from £670 freehold.

A model house would be erected to the purchaser's own design on a selected site and the purchase money could be paid by the payment down of a deposit and the balance secured over a period of years as rent.

Plots of land can also be acquired upon the same advantageous terms. The purchase is also free from Surveyor's and legal charges, with the exception of stamps, registration and out of pocket disbursements.

There is a direct entry and exit from the Pinner Railway Station on to the Estate which is open for the convenience of residents during the busy hours of the day.

Both electric light and gas services are installed.

Local rates are exceptionally low being only 5/2 in the £.

Full particulars can be obtained of :—

H. GIBSON,
Metropolitan Railway General Offices,
'Phone Mayfair 6640.   **BAKER STREET STATION.**

In answering advertisements, please mention " METRO-LAND.*"*

80

25M—1/5/16

Right: The Cecil Park Estate, Pinner, was developed by the Surplus Lands Committee in the 1890s and 1900s, and offered high quality residences far removed from the smoke of London, yet conveniently placed for frequent trains to Baker Street.

Below: The forecourt of Pinner station in the 1930s, complete with pebble-dashed Estate Office, offered properties for sale or rent in the adjacent Cecil Park. The location of estate agents' offices in this way became a common feature of stations on the extension line. [1998/55975]

Above: The Ruislip Manor estate on the Uxbridge line was developed on land owned by the local council and provided with a basic wooden halt in 1912. House-building was halted by the First World War and did not restart until the late 1920s. [1998/54590]

Right: Robert Hope Selbie, General Manager of the Metropolitan from 1908 until his death in 1930. A man of untiring drive and commitment, Selbie came to personify the Met and dominate the Board. His principal aim was to increase revenue, mainly by developing commuter traffic along the sparsely populated extension line. To achieve this, he first implemented improvements to the existing infrastructure (including rebuilding Baker Street station) and reorganised estate management and publicity. With these foundations in place, the Metropolitan was able to intensify the programme of estate development, which led to the creation of Metro-land. [1998/40809]

One of the major preparatory civil engineering works was the installation of express tracks between Finchley Road and Wembley Park, from 1913-15. This resulted in the construction of a new steel girder bridge at Kilburn in 1915, next to the original railway bridge (just visible on the left of the picture). It was designed by the Metropolitan's Chief Engineer, William Willox, and carries the full title of the company in painted panels on each side.

Metro-Land, 1920. The first edition of the *Metro-Land* guidebook was published in 1915. It was lavishly produced with several colour plates extolling the virtues of the rural areas served by the railway. It was also the first time that the term 'Metro-land' appeared in print. Over the next seventeen years, 'Metro-land' entered the language as a shorthand term for the districts north west of London in Middlesex, Hertfordshire and Buckinghamshire. Unlike other railway guidebooks, *Metro-Land* promoted both leisure travel and home-ownership, and later had an extensive 'House Seekers' section.

The Metropolitan Railway war memorial at Baker Street, commemorating the 137 employees killed on active service. It was designed by the Company architect, C.W. Clark, and unveiled by Lord Aberconway on Armistice Day 1920. [1998/38329]

Female staff outside the Company's headquarters in Allsop Place during the First World War. Women were recruited from 1915 to fill jobs vacated by men volunteering for the Armed Services. The war necessarily caused a postponement of Selbie's plans for residential development, although the vision of Metro-land as a bright, healthy, alternative to inner London was to gain considerable emotional weight following the end of hostilities in 1918. [2004/1547]

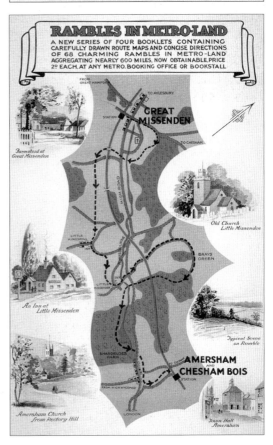

'A Tour Through Metro-Land', 1921. As part of the Metro-land advertising campaign, the MRCE organised special tours for the press.

Right: Leisure travel, golf, fishing, country walks and rambles in Metro-land were all used to promote the area as both a place to visit and a place to live.

Opposite above: Ellesborough church – a typical photograph from Metro-land presenting a sentimental portrayal of Englishness that was to prove to be very successful in selling houses. Metro-land housing never reached this far and Ellesborough remains largely unchanged today. [2002/12090]

Opposite below: Homes 'fit for heroes': the Cedars Estate, between Rickmansworth and Chorley Wood, was one of the first to be developed by the Metropolitan Railway Country Estates Limited (MRCE), formed in 1919 to accelerate the programme of line-side property development. Officially an independent undertaking, the MRCE was directed by the Met and had its offices at Baker Street.

Above: 'Ancient thatched cottages near Aylesbury' – another carefully selected image of Old England from the pages of *Metro-Land*, promising a 'rural Arcadia close to London'. [2002/11668]

Right: The advertising campaign even extended to carriage door handles which from the mid-1920s carried the slogan, 'Live in Metro-Land'.

A school group returning from a day trip to rural Eastcote in 1925. The Pleasure Gardens and Pavilion at Eastcote were a favourite destination for school parties in the 1920s, with up to 3,000 passengers using the station on busy days. By the early thirties the area had been transformed by new housing estates. [1998/79674]

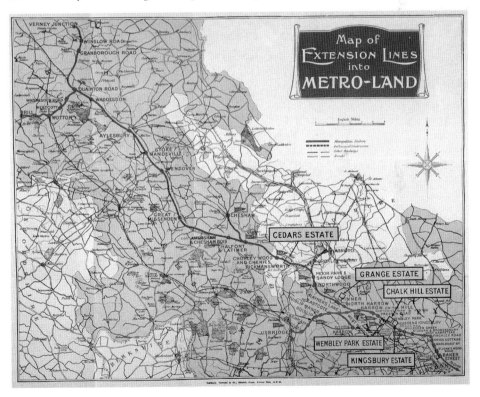

A map showing the principal MRCE estates in 1924. With the exception of the Cedars Estate, the earliest developments were clustered in northwest London at Wembley, Neasden and Kingsbury. As the decade progressed, the focus shifted to the Uxbridge branch and main line as far north as Amersham, with private developers plugging many of the gaps in between.

Northwick Park station opened in 1923 to serve a new residential development. Continued house building in the area, including the MRCE Northwick Estate, led to the station being enlarged and rebuilt in 1931. [1998/65319]

Motive power for Metro-land. From 1925, passenger travel on the extension line was provided by electric traction as far as Rickmansworth and steam thereafter. [1998/87310]

Above: The only intermediate station on the rural Uxbridge branch when it opened in 1904, Ruislip became a focus for suburban growth in the 1920s. The MRCE developed two estates near the station at Manor Farm (nineteen and a half acres) and Elm Grove (twenty-one and a half acres). [1999/20741]

Right: An MRCE publication advertising Ruislip as 'the most accessible and the least spoiled of the residential districts around London'. The cover illustration is typical of the larger mock Tudor houses to be found in Metro-land. Inside, the intending resident could find information on local rates, gas supply, places of worship, banks and schools.

RUISLIP

AT LAST—A 'QUALITY' HOUSE AT LOW COST

HERE is your chance—seize it! A real worth-while "quality" seven-room house for £695 Freehold. No road charges, no legal costs, and no stamp fees to pay! Built of the finest materials; thoughtfully planned; excellently appointed, with rooms throughout that possess that cheery touch of brightness that means everything. Inner fittings and equipment include—totally enclosed porcelain enamelled bath; magnificent tiled fireplaces; chromium plated fittings throughout; beautifully tiled kitchens and bathrooms; constant hot water supply; electric fittings and shades, etc., etc.

The Ruislip Station Estate, on which these delightful houses are located, has everything in its favour. It can be

£695
FREEHOLD

reached, from Town, in less time than it takes to read your evening paper. On all sides are green fields and pleasant hedgerows. The climate is mild and equable; the air is healthy and invigorating, whilst unlimited facilities for outdoor recreation obtain and particularly liberal educational and shopping facilities exist.

Why not go further into the matter—it will pay you! Write to-day, or telephone Ruislip 217 or 626, for free travelling voucher from any London station and for illustrated descriptive booklet. The houses can be inspected any day, including Sundays, and our representatives, who are always available, will readily answer any question or explain any point without the slightest obligation on your part to buy.

H. L. BOWERS, RUISLIP STATION ESTATE, MIDDX.

Above: Stylish, modern and fast, the 1921 Met-Vickers locomotives encapsulated the Metro-land dream. From 1927, all twenty locomotives received names relating to figures or (in the case of *Wembley 1924*) places associated with Metro-land. No.19 was named after the medieval church reformer, *John Wycliffe*. [1998/64441]

Opposite above: Hillingdon was opened in 1923 in readiness for the expected boom in suburban building along the Uxbridge branch. In its first year, ticket receipts barely covered operational expenses, yet by 1930 the station was taking over £12,000 thanks to residential developments on both sides of the line. [1998/81679]

Opposite below: A 1932 Metro-land advert for 'low cost' housing on the Bowers estate next to Ruislip Station. House prices varied considerably between estates, from £650 for a modest bungalow in Wembley to over £2,000 for a detached house on the prestigious Cedars Estate at Rickmansworth.

Above and below: The original street level booking hall and basic wooden platforms of Rayners Lane halt. It opened in 1906 to encourage local development and was later the junction for District Railway trains to Hammersmith and London. Despite this, the area remained largely rural until the arrival of speculative builders in the late 1920s. [1998/64441 and 1998/88719]

A 1929 poster advertising Harrow Garden Village, adjacent to Rayners Lane station. The 213-acre site was developed by E.S. Reid and became the most immediately successful of all the MRCE estates. Houses cost from £895 to £1,350.

A GOOD MOVE

— TO HARROW GARDEN VILLAGE

21 MINUTES FROM BAKER STREET. HOUSES OF VARYING TYPE BUILT BY WELL-KNOWN BUILDERS AVAILABLE AT POPULAR PRICES. LIBERAL OPEN SPACES, TENNIS COURTS, ETC. EXCELLENT SITES FOR HOUSES AND SHOP PLOTS IN COMMANDING POSITIONS. FULL PARTICULARS FROM H. GIBSON, GENERAL OFFICES, BAKER ST. STATION.NW1 CHEAP TICKETS FROM ALL METRO. STATIONS ON THURSDAYS, SATURDAYS AND SUNDAYS TO RAYNERS LANE (FOR HARROW GARDEN VILLAGE) ADJOINING ESTATE

LIVE ON THE WELLER ESTATE AMERSHAM

The Weller Estate at Amersham (1930) was the most northerly to be developed by the MRCE. The 78-acre site consisted of 535 semi-detached houses served by fifty-one shops.

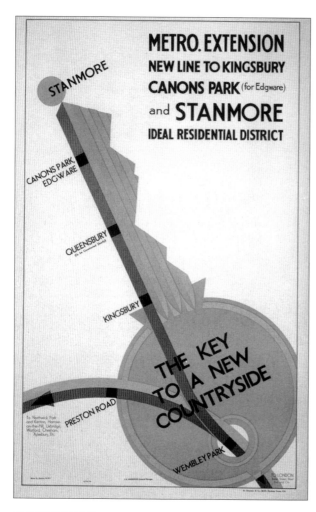

METRO. EXTENSION
NEW LINE TO KINGSBURY
CANONS PARK (for Edgware)
and **STANMORE**
IDEAL RESIDENTIAL DISTRICT

Left: The Key To A New Countryside, 1932. The four-mile branch line from Wembley to Stanmore was the Metropolitan's last extension. It was promoted by landowners eager to capitalise on the boom in suburban building. The Met was also keen to populate the area with season ticket holders, especially as railway construction costs could be offset by government subsidies designed to relieve unemployment.

Below: Kingsbury station on the Stanmore branch in 1932. Even before the station was opened, house building was well advanced. Within a year the vacant plots next to the station would be built on and the area transformed into a new suburb with its own shopping centre and cinema. [1998/81995]

Opposite: The inaugural train on the Stanmore branch in Kingsbury cutting on 9 December 1932. [1998/86515]

Above and below: The station building and platforms at Stanmore, designed by C.W. Clark in 1933. The station closely resembled his earlier work for the Watford branch and reflected the domestic architecture of the estates it served. [1999/7230 and 1999/20751]

Above: New acres for Metro-land: A notice announces the 'Site for a New Station' at the railway bridge on rural Joel Street, near Northwood, c.1931. A competition was held to find a suitable name for the station and the subsequent housing development, which became known as Northwood Hills. [2004/2]

Below: The same view in 1936, showing the completed railway station and terrace of new shops and houses. About 3,000 homes were eventually built on the estate. [1998/55930]

Northwood Hills in 1934. This was the last station built by the Met. Designed by C.W. Clark, it incorporated an estate agent's office for the rapidly growing suburb. [1998/55935]

Homes in Metro-Land: a London Transport poster from 1933. LT quickly dropped the Metro-land slogan, which did not appear after 1933. The MRCE and Surplus Lands Committee both outlived the Metropolitan as independent companies and were still active in the 1950s.

six

Metropolitan London

Above: The passenger entrance to Moorgate station on Moorfields Road, redesigned by George Campbell Sherrin in the 1890s. Offices, known as Moorgate Chambers, were built above the station in 1902-03. The building was severely damaged by air raids during the Second World War and later demolished. [1998/69258]

Left: Moorgate station parcels office, photographed in the mid-1930s. The Metropolitan operated its own parcels and local delivery service in central London from 1890. [1999/29099]

Above: Paddington (Praed Street) in the 1930s. The brick retaining walls are almost completely obscured by advertising hoardings, in a scene that would have been typical of many Met stations on the Circle line. [1998/71012]

Right: The red and blue diamond-shaped logo adopted for publicity in 1914 and used on station nameboards from 1915. The design was influenced by the bar and circle roundel of the Underground Group. A green version was used on the East London Railway after 1923, in deference to the Southern Railway. The diamond logo was most associated with central and suburban London, and rarely replaced conventional nameboards on the northern reaches of the extension line. [1998/57493]

The epitome of Metropolitan style and aspiration – the rebuilt Baker Street station after completion in 1930. The main building was dominated by a block of luxury flats, named Chiltern Court, while adjacent offices housed the headquarters of the company. Architecturally, Clark's neo-Georgian façade gave the structure an Edwardian appearance, which was in keeping with the solid, slightly conservative, values of the railway. [1998/88562]

Opposite above: The entrance to Baker Street station on Marylebone Road, c.1914. The station and junction with the extension line was completely rebuilt between 1912 and 1930. The first phase included alterations to the track layout and the construction of an elevated approach road serving a new ticket hall (seen here) finished in Portland stone. [1999/21013]

Opposite below: The bronze memorial plaque on Marylebone Road recording the laying of the foundation stone for the new Baker Street station by Lord Aberconway on 24 July 1912. A more modest plaque below commemorates the 1963 centenary of the Metropolitan. [1998/66108]

The extension line platforms at Baker Street, showing the back of Chiltern Court (centre) and company offices (left) on 23 August 1938. The rebuilt station occupied a triangle of land bounded by Marylebone Road, Upper Baker Street and Allsop Place, and included the site of the former Baker Street East station. In this photograph, an electric train pulls away north, while a 1921 Metro-Vick engine stands in the loco siding (centre, left). [1998/66301]

A busy scene at Baker Street parcels depot, c.1930. A central sorting office was first opened here in 1893. By the mid-1920s the Met was handling over 850,000 parcels a year. A large fleet of horse-drawn and motor vans was maintained for this service, with stables at Loveridge Road, Kilburn. [1998/88693]

Farringdon and High Holborn was the first of several central area stations to be remodelled and modernised during the 1920s. Designed by C.W. Clark, the station was finished in white faience, with the company title in red lettering. This view was taken shortly after the work was completed in November 1923. [1998/81006]

Edgware Road station was completely reconstructed between 1926-28. The works included alteration to the track layout, re-signalling, and a new surface building with residential flats on the first floor. The total cost came to £118,000. [1998/58318]

THE **CHILTERN COURT**
RESTAURANT
BAKER STREET STATION

*Perfect Cuisine
and
Faultless Service*

NOW OPEN

Above: A 250-seat restaurant opened at Chiltern Court, Baker Street, in November 1929. Run by the railway buffet caterers, Spiers & Pond, and decorated in an unfashionable Edwardian style, it failed to attract the smart clientele that its expenditure required.

Opposite above: Rebuilding on a smaller scale took place at Swiss Cottage from 1928-29. Clark's design included a new entrance leading to an arcade of shops with flats above. [1998/49074]

Opposite below: Great Portland Street was among the last of the central area stations to be rebuilt by Clarke, 1929-30. The two-storey elliptical surface building stands on an island site and originally incorporated several shops and a motor showroom. [1998/70043]

Above: A new corporate identity for the Metropolitan line: Euston Square station with London Transport roundel and signage in July 1935. The creation of LT in 1933 saw the gradual re-branding of ex-Metropolitan stations, although some retained the red diamond name signs into the 1950s. [1998/70005]

Opposite above: The last coal train to Chiltern Court, photographed at Baker Street on its return journey with the open wagon behind the locomotive filled with rubbish in 1961. Boiler coal had been delivered to the flats in this way, and refuse removed, since Chiltern Court opened in 1929. [1998/55883]

Opposite below: An illustration of a typical drawing room in one of the larger flats, Chiltern Court publicity brochure, 1929. There were 198 flats in total, plus a block of thirty bedrooms for maids. Rents ranged from £1,000 a year for ten-room 'mansion flats' to £250 for a three-room 'bachelor flat'. Early tenants included the authors H.G. Wells and Arnold Bennett.

Other local titles published by Tempus

The Willing Servant A History of the Steam Locomotive
DAVID ROSS

Taking us through the last two hundred years, David Ross tells not just the story of the steam engine but also of its effects on mankind. From small beginnings, the railway locomotive was responsible for the speed of industrialisation in many countries, for commuting, for tourism, for industrial progress in all fields and for making the people of the world a transient workforce. Without it, the world would be a different place.
0 7524 2986 8

London's Railways
KEN SCHOLEY

London's Railways gives a unique insight into the history of the railways in Britain's capital city. This book brings the classic age of rail travel to life and demonstrates to its readers just how much London was, and still is, dependent on the shimmering ribbons of steel that have penetrated both over and under the city from all directions. A fascinating read for everyone; commuters, locals and tourists.
0 7524 1605 7

London's River From Westminster to Woolwich
CHRIS THURMAN

One man's photographic record of the Thames from the 1960s to the present day. The river Thames has been the lifeblood of London since before Roman times. It is its raison d'être and has been responsible for the growth of this remarkable city. This book captures the many changes along the river over the last forty years.
0 7524 2595 1

London Life in the Post-War Years
DOUGLAS WHITWORTH

A photographic chronicle of London after 1945. This is a collection of evocative photographs taken in London in the immediate post-war years, showing some of the best-known sights in the capital, including Blitz damage, Oxford Street shop windows, the Festival of Britain and the Coronation decorations.
0 7524 2816 0

If you are interested in purchasing other books published by Tempus, or in case you have difficulty finding any Tempus books in your local bookshop, you can also place orders directly through our website

www.tempus-publishing.com